Women, Men and Country
An Anthology of African Poems

Peagie Woobay, Stockholm 2013

Copyright © 2013 by Khadi Mansaray
All rights reserved. This book or any portion thereof may not be reproduced or used in any manner whatsoever without the express written permission of the publisher or contributors except for the use of brief quotations in a book review or scholarly journal.
Second Printing: 2013
ISBN-13: 978-1493684298

ISBN-10: 1493684299

Khadi Mansaray

London, United Kingdom

Dedication

I dedicate these poems to The Girl Child of Sierra Leone, so that they will stay in school and become successful women.

Women, Men and Country: An Anthology of African Poems

Compiled by Khadi Mansaray
Foreword by Isha Sesay, CNN Anchor

Khadi Mansaray
2013

Contents

Acknowledgements ix
Foreword xi
Preface xiii
Introduction xv
Part I: Conscience 17

    A Seed does not bear fruit over night
    The Apothecary
    Others
    Babbling Foetus
    Nowhere To Run To
    Bear With Me
    Barbed Wire
    The Window
    Gangs of Bandits
    They Call it Culture
    Whats the name of the game?
    Confessions
    Peace
    Managed Directly by God
    In the name of God
    Am I my Sister's Keeper?
    Infinity
    Freedom Fighters
    Cup of Agbo
    Democracy
    Violence in Silence
    My Mother Does Not Know
    Mystery World of Mystery People

Part II: WOMEN 49

    For Valerie
    Woman
    I Hear A Woman Cry
    Our Pains, Our World
    Dreams of a Girl
    A Sense of Direction
    A Beauty, A Mother, A Mentor
    I Refuse
    Dance of Life
    This Poem is For Her
    Educating A Girl Child
    The Eyes of A Woman
    The Strength of A Woman
    The Tears of A Woman
    The Smiles of A Woman
    Elegance
    Her Beauty
    Stirred
    Undefined

Part III: MEN 69

    Men
    My Heart o' mine
    Am I A Boy?
    Grandfather
    The Superior Race

Part IV: COUNTRY 79

    Horizontal Green White and Blue
    Our Own Place
    The Place
    Land That We Love
    Mena Hills
    Sierra Leone, The Beauty of a Nation
    The Lion
    The Flag of Sierra Leone
    My Land! My Home! My Country!
    Bunce Island

    Nelson Mandela
    Unconventional?
    Managed Directly by God from Heaven
    Memories of 28

Part V: HAIKU CORNER 93

    Salone
    The Land
    The Sea
    The Wind
    Love

MEET THE POETS 95

    Abdul Tejan Cole
    Abibatu Samura
    Achieng Achena
    Ade Daramy
    Agnes K Dugba Macauley
    Akwasi Aidoo
    Chadia Talib
    Claudia Anthony
    David E Manley
    Dawah Sese Koker
    Eldred D Jones
    Fatou Wurie
    Festy Natty
    Fouad Ayoub
    Foyre Jalloh
    Isata Mahoi
    Janice Williams
    Josephine Coker
    Khadi Mansaray
    Linda Ochiel
    Marie Fornah
    Milton Margai
    Osman Sankoh
    Rahmatullah Mansaray
    Roland Marke
    Zeena Hamady

Acknowledgements

As always, they have supported me, given me a second chance, of which I made very good use. I want to thank my parents for their unending support, my siblings and friends and even those who I have never met, but who have just believed in The Peagie Woobay Dream. I thank you all.

Peagie Woobay

This wonderful collection would not have happened without the contributions from the poets who believed in the cause and supported it. Special thanks to the poets from Ghana and Kenya who choose to support us, Conrad Lisk and Saidu K Sesay for patiently reading every draft and helping me "kill my darlings" and Abdul Tejan-Cole for supporting the Peagie Woobay Scholarship Fund, being my sounding board and for those valuable introductions. My family and friends who remind me to write every year and support everything I do, but most of all Professor and Mrs Jones who looked at my first poems all those years ago and encouraged me to write more. Lastly my heartfelt thanks go to everyone who simply believed in me.

Khadi Mansaray

Foreword

Life and career have taken me around the world, but Sierra Leone will always be home for me. My family moved from London to Freetown when I was seven years old and for much of my formative years, it was a place filled with love, light and laughter. I grew up feeling strong and confident, unafraid of the world beyond my front door. Looking back, my sense of empowerment didn't just come from my parents. It was also because of the society as a whole. I remember it as a time when girls felt valued, schools like St. Joseph's Secondary and Annie Walsh were reputable centres of learning. There was a feeling of hope and infinite possibilities…

Much has changed since my early years in Freetown; instability and war ripped apart the lives and dreams of millions over the course of the 90s. And the rate of teenage pregnancy in Sierra Leone skyrocketed. All too often these girls who find themselves pregnant are pushed to the margins of society and left to flounder hopelessly. This is why The Peagie Woobay Scholarship Fund is so important; it provides a lifeline for teenage mothers, by giving them the chance to go back to school. The fund allows these young girls to dream and work towards a life out of the shadows. At the same time, the fund promotes education and highlights the dangers that accompany teenage pregnancies.

This beautiful collection of poetry will transport you to another time and place. The reality of Sierra Leone's brutal civil war; the abducted girls, scattered families and lives forever changed is brought home in these verses. There is pain and sorrow, but there is also strength. Themes of female fortitude, faith and looking to the future are also explored and serve as a reminder of that universal truth – the human spirit can overcome any obstacle.

Rich with imagery and emotion these poems will haunt you. But more than that, I hope you will be inspired to reach out and help lift up Sierra Leone's girls. I believe every girl child should grow up with a feeling of hope and infinite possibilities – just like I did…

Isha Sesay, CNN Anchor
October 2013

Preface

Peagie Woobay was my senior years ago at the Annie Walsh Memorial School, but I actually got to know her better on Facebook. Her interest in women's empowerment led me to invite her to be a panelist on Voices from the Diaspora, a radio show I host and she became the star of that edition. She inspired us all by sharing her personal experience of teenage pregnancy and her dream of helping others who may find themselves in similar situations.

Many people help empower girls in various ways but Peagie stood out because she was reaching out to a group that did not usually get sympathy. In a society that can be judgmental and unforgiving, it was courageous for her to openly and boldly tell her story. Her candor was disarming and her sincerity was contagious. Being a business coach I wanted to help the charity improve its operations and raise funds. Peagie and I shared another interest, Poetry. Her 'Woman' series is the inspiration for this collection and her private collection forms the core of the book. I also come across beautiful poems written by Africans and I thought it would be wonderful to get them all together for such a worthy cause. The response has been overwhelming and gone beyond borders of Sierra Leone. Contributions range from budding talent as young as sixteen to veterans like Professor Eldred Jones, who encouraged me to write as young as eleven. The result is a rich, diverse collection. I am deeply honored that every poet believed in the cause enough to entrust their works to me.

Introduction

The collection is split into five categories. In Conscience, you find poems that provoke thought. They make you stop and think. They may wrench your heart or simply inspire you.

The sections Women, Men, Country take their name from the title. Poems about Women celebrate womanhood. They give a glimpse into the mysterious depths of our souls and tell of our joys and sorrows. They also include verses from men who recognise our invaluable contribution to society.

The poems in Men recognise that men and women are always linked whether in harmony or conflict. These poems explore the turbulent emotions of this bond and the ultimate acceptance of that relationship.

In Country you find love letters to Sierra Leone from patriots around the world. Sierra Leoneans and visitors alike fall in love with its beauty. These poems celebrate the uneasy but enduring love we have for our country.

Finally, haiku poems, originally from Japan, have been around since the 9th century. They are short and use sensory language to capture the moment. Contemporary haikus do not abide to the strict Japanese format, however they are still short and punchy and give deeper meaning to physical things. The ideal poetry for the Twitter generation, they describe images, and emotions in a few words. I love haikus or maybe I'm just too lazy to write ballads!
Welcome to Women, Men and Country. I hope you enjoy.

Part I: Conscience

A Seed Doesn't Bear Fruit Overnight
by Milton Margai

I want books
Not babies at this stage.
I want to go to school
Not a marital home.
I need a teacher
Not a husband.
I want my childhood
Not ready for 'adulthood'.
A seed doesn't bear fruit overnight
Only when the time is right.
Prepare me and I'll blossom
At the right time.
Give me books and send me to school
And I'll be the mother
You want me to be.

The Apothecary by Festy Natty

Temptation sports a transparent thong,
but doesn't advertise
when we avert eyes,
Salacity as strong
as pungent fulmination
or refulgent illumination;

Focus is the apothecary who prescribes
Discipline the antidote
that will amply coat
him with armour that describes
picture of immunity
with cultured impunity

Others by Abdul Tejan Cole

We were at par
Together sweating for the Bar.
I was clouted in the spar.
Today, his racing car
Has left me behind, by far.

He was my mate
Together we sought success' gate.
They say it's Ill fate
On the day, he arrived late
Today he is down to fourth rate
Sitting by the river with an empty bait.

Babbling Foetus
by Claudia Anthony

On my path, long, long path
I hear sounds, as I bath
children on playgrounds singing,
music in the distance playing.
Tyres screech, horns blast,
plates the table slap fast
food is ready I'd cook one day,
said I to myself one fine day.
Father's home, toys with my mat
listen to my voice, beams like cat
so I give him a kick, have a laugh
he too, a hard, long laugh.
Mother smiles, broad beaming,
I'm wise, can feel, yes can sing
but they can't tell; they don't know.
One more month and nine 'ld blow;
then can I real cuddle have,
see playgrounds, tyres; observe
the kitchen, and all those cars
which that noisy world offers.
But behold!
Doctor in stinking combat
as if camped in forgotten drought,
step in my path and tear my mat.
With cutlass, dull be it feat
force me out and back I beat
before my first breath I take.
This is my fate when evil men
even life undue take!

Nowhere To Run To
by Claudia Anthony

Behold my City!
itself sunning peacefully,
sunshine soaking up!
Lo! Petrified janitor;
church bells don't chime
nor choir hymns sing,
or preacher sermon preach
in my City.

Children of my City starve
the sick, many die;
yet for cover, the strong duck
while howling dogs cover seek
as roofs blow apart
by flying wingless cartridges
on a Sunday,
in my City.

Bear With Me by Fatou Wurie

Bear with me
Bear with me
Bear with me
Teday teday teday
Mama yooooooooo
Den dey cam den dey cam
Mama den dey cam
Den dey cam
My dreams are still realities
That nestle in profanities
As I smell blood they extract
From limbs in deadened streams
The red sea cries
As Babylon sails
But I'm in salone
Sweet sweet salone
Teday
Where assailed voices don't pass Freetown
So I'm asking freed slaves
come chain me
take me away
Freed slaves
Come chain me
and take me away
To a land where pain isn't gain
And rain isn't placed into the fast lane
Of destruction

Maaama yoo
Mamama yooooo
Sweet salone
Den dey de diee ohhhhhhhhh
My mother's bosom warm with security
Rocks me back and forth
Forth and back
Gestating me back to reality

Khadi Mansaray

But my body has memory
The day they divided my legs
They forced my honeycomb to burst
Shot papa
I say I dey yerie yerie
Uncle done run away
To green bushes
Mama mama cam cam cam
So mam rocks me to the present, present, present
Be here in the present
She soothes and says
na dream you dey dream dream deam
But it feels so damn real
This might be my last meal
paradise don gone
na sweet sweet salone

See people ask me all the time isn't it the place
where diamonds reside?
How is it going by the way?
Last time I checked it wasn't safe
You know, like there are problems there

Women, Men and Country

Where were you when they asked me
Short sleeve or long sleeve
Asked me to love a part of me
Where were you
When they bitched slapped me
And asked raped or pounded
My dear which will you be
Where were you
When they burnt
Houses down
Where were you when they burnt
schools down
Intellects and judges down
Children and brightened dreams downs

Disempowered minds
Political turnarounds
Left all of us in the dogpound so
Bear with me when I cry in the night
Bear with me if I'm still angry deep in side
Bear with me if I smoke to escape
Or if I drink to daydream
Peacefully..
Bear with me when I freak out in bed
Bear with me when my heart violates to be heard
Bear with me when I screaaaam
Sweet salone salone
Bear with me
Stories are spilling
Sweet salone salone
Bear with me

Khadi Mansaray

Death is still grieving
den say den day den say salone pickin
wona cam back cam back cam back
salone pickin
wona came back
wona forget forget
wona forget forgive
bear with me
if I can't forget
bear with me
If I can't forgive
For My body has memory

Bear with me
Bear with me
Bear with me

Barbed Wire by Fouad Ayoub

My heart feels like it's been choked with barbed wire,
while my breath slowly departs my lungs,
escaping from the bars of my aching ribcage.
A heart that's like a rose,
smooth petals curled up to hide the atrocities that lies inside.
My hand trembles,my heart beats,
my eyes weep and I cannot think.
You've haunted my memories and captured my mind,
oh God,how can I break free.

The Window
By Christopher Dawah Sese Koker

I looked through the Window
And what did I see
A multitude of people
Roaming the valley below

Where are all these People
Going, I don't know
Or should I know
So I could let them Know ?

Then It dawned on me
The Window was foggy
I should have Known
Blinds drawn very low

How can a window be so cold
Framed under a ceiling way so high
To give a view that could be clear
Then I remembered the people where not bold

Enough to notice the house
Sitting high up the Mountain
Was theirs to own
Left alone to be blown by the wind of time.

Gang of Bandits by Claudia Anthony

mental, physical your light they steal
your health, your sight, your taste,
the gang!

gaggles you, your breath, your smell
your sounds and lo! stands you as mute
the gang!

sweet-talks you of bridges never built,
while many a road lie awkward in tilt
the gang!

Shows off, see them like perennial princes!
ride carriages their monies can't buy
the gang!

lives in palace for which you pay dearly
red carpets catwalks in white flowing gowns
the gang!

Be it tobacco leaves* 'round necks hang
now tread they on your backs hard
the gang!

from dawn till dusk robs and loots
safes they sweep clean that which's yours
the gang!

reeks power and riches; yea! The bank's broke
now serve you them not the reverse
the gang!

years speed, again there's knock on your door
brings lies of bridges that'll never be built
the gang!

*   tobacco leaf (leaves) – Krio slang for necktie (s)

They Call It Culture by Claudia Anthony

Some were told a woman they'ld be
If initiated into a secret society
Where, they'ld learn a woman to be
And be ripe their offspring to raise.

I wasn't told why I should've been there
When at tender nine a cut so severe,
With blade and days profusely bled and
Pained from age-old coercion of males.

Some were told a good wife they'ld be
Free from that they labelled promiscuity;
Serve husbands in faith; rivals compare,
Say mates: same husband coition share.

I wasn't told I would orgasms hardly get;
Whole life I'ld copulate without the joy
Suffer from years I wished I wasn't cut
And leap about like frog in search of joy.

What's The Name Of The Game?
by Claudia Anthony

The mouse confided in the cat
There was huge order from cows
The cat whispered to the dog
There was titanic hunters' windfall

The three settled down to play
With wads of bills contracts offer
For projects to develop their land
But which kick off waned of goal

In return the mouse got stipends
To educate his pack of mice abroad
The cat in its turn got barrels of milk
To feed her six kwashiorkor kittens

At day's end the mouse chewed up
Lots of files to incapacitate the trap
The dog boned his puppies' kennel
And the three in kickbacks revelled

Confessions by David E Manley

*Bless me father for I have sinned
it's been ages since my last confession
I have left my first love by the wayside
Allowed my feelings to grow lukewarm
neither too hot to be bothered
nor too cold to give up completely...
My first love remains certain
Her colors still breed peace in her gentle sway
Her song still brings tears to grown men's eyes...
but no longer do I stand and salute her colors
no longer do I sing out loud her song...
no longer am I called hers
 From this day henceforth father
I promise to start anew.
Promise to rekindle the love that first drew me in
Promise to salute the swaying green white and blue
Promise to belt out loud
from my bottommost heart
with tear-filled eyes
her exaltations lifted high
Filled with pride to be called hers and hers alone
Promise to always be true to her
Feet firmly planted in her
Always roaming
Never leaving
Her name always in my heart
Her looks forever etched on mine
Till the day we're finally united in love*

Peace by David E Manley

*Silent yet speaking volumes,
The ripples set forth.
Further and further
Away from the bank,
On a journey
Towards the deep.
Where lies buried
The secrets
Throughout the ages.
Our sons and daughters
Claimed by the sea.
The knowledge,
Lost in the sands
Mirroring the infinity
Of the galaxy alive.
And as they move
Further and further away
They forever whisper
Peace.
Peace within me
I and the universe are one.
Peace around me,
The wind tickles the sand
Caresses the water and
Seduces the sky.
As the ripples flow
further and further away
They cart the worries with them
Until all I'm left with ,
Is Peace.*

In the name of God by Linda Ochiel

Perhaps some day the sun will shine again,
And we shall see that still the skies are blue
Above the West Gate
That you went through
And was never seen again
So we are bereft of you…
And may live in vain, forever

Perhaps the rescue team will find you alive
Give you water and shelter you to safety
The brave men and women
That have put lives on line
To bring you back home
In one piece

Perhaps the sun will shimmer bright tomorrow,
Over the billowing smoke at Gate in the Waste
From where we wonder whether your saintly soul
Is here or gone
With every deafening explosion
Of fierce guns and consuming fire

You did attend the cookery competition
At the Gate in the West, right?
So how did you end up in the mound of the lifeless?
You promised to bring a winning prize home, right?
Or did you loose?
But why did you not come back to home
To mama to console you?

Angel
Even in a fierce quarrel of guns
Such horrific mangle of humanity and rubbles
Your resilient spirit gives us
HOPE and FORTITUDE

'But though kind time may many joys renew
There is one greatest joy we shall not know
Again, because our heart for loss of You'
Senselessly in the hand of
Heartless cowards
Pushing an imprudent agenda
In the name of God

Am I My Sister's Keeper by Ade Daramy

Yes, that is my sister
The one with the smiling face in the picture above the fireplace
She's not here as we had to leave her 'back there'.

I remember the day like it was yesterday
How we were so proud as we joined the rest of the crowd
Right to the edge of town to the place where men were not allowed

As she smiled and waved, I couldn't help but ponder what I'd told her
How I would always be her protector
And I asked myself Am I my sister's keeper?

I can remember when mum said this had always been the plan
You leave here a girl and come back a woman
I just have to say my girl, I've long waited for this day

For some reason I remember the clear, blue sky and
The way the noise was pierced by my mother's cry
"Why did they have to take my girl, Why?"

Every word said was like a dagger in my heart
I never thought this was how we would part

She's been taken by the ancestors, one woman said
"If they had to take someone why not the old woman instead?"
For my insolence I got a whack around the head.

As we began to grieve, we could scarcely believe
Another family heard the news: their girl had been 'taken', too

"These things happen; there's really nothing we could do"

They call it tradition, and part of our history
The way of these things have always been a mystery
Some saw it as fate and not a cause fro misery.

The day I left, as the rage inside me burned
I swore I never would return
A million ancestors could not pull me back to walk along that familiar track

Do we live for tradition or die by it?
Do we learn from the past or are we tied to it?
Do we have to do all that our ancestors did?

As I recall that smile again
I recall the hurt, anger and the pain
I remember my promise to protect her
Could I have been my sister's keeper?

Yes, that is my sister
The one with the smiling face in the picture above the fireplace
She's not here as we had to leave her 'back there'.

Infinity by Achieng Maureen Akena

*It doesn't stop, it just keeps going
round and round and round again
like a bottomless pot of magic*

*It doesn't stop, it just keeps going
round and round and round again
like love that never dies*

*It doesn't stop, it just keeps going
round and round and round again
like lives intertwined in time*

*It doesn't stop, it just keeps going
round and round and round again
like troubles that never cease*

*It doesn't stop, it just keeps going
round and round and round again
like pain that never ends*

*It doesn't stop, it just keeps going
round and round and round again
like the angst of separation*

*It doesn't stop, it just keeps going
round and round and round again*

like the ring on my finger

Freedom Fighters by Khadi Mansaray

They came to free us
Or so they said
The crops are burnt
The cattle dead
Daughters raped
Husbands killed
Sons fled
The land is bare
But they came to free us
Or so they said

Cup of Agbo by Roland Marke

Indignity gobbles a resentful cup of agbo mixture
As oppression's mental chains scar-tissue rupture.

Redemption from scorpion whips, at summer-heat
Tenor of hope chants victory of ancestral heartbeat.

I spectate in wide-eye wonder the unhallowed fame
Tsunami storm ravaged through my ancestral dome.

Judas nursed reproach on beloved Christian name
Lust to gain: imbued action without fear or shame.

Ignoble, pious hands loathe for banal human hold
And barter amiable souls for impure ounce of gold.

As teary, shrinking eyes, mystic testament evolves
Conscience of morality honed mire disenchantment.

Could valor restitute illumination amid roar of tide?
As love plummets, God's purpose soon soar us ride.

Soon, stoop the conqueror beneath the conquered
Noon droop, Freetown's a Mecca of souls expired.

Democracy by Roland Marke

Music in democracy's soothing as it is healing,
And it involuntarily moves my mouth to salivate.
Harmonious chorus jumpstarts awe, inspiration:
Christiana, the lead musician, serves the need.
She goads guilded soloists to save the harmony,
And to herald unification's fountain of equality:
Songs of Mendes, Creoles, Temnes, Limbas --
A mélange of melodies that might save the world.
Late Siaka Stevens said: democracies see us as
Sierra Leoneans, not chucks of tribal divisions.
Strangers, whisper, I like your romantic accent.
Many think Africa's just a country, no continent.
I dance to democracy's stride, in Sierra Leone.
A chord of music that melts as it merges hearts.
Birth pains: symptoms of an emerging democracy.
To replay our dire history, only invites the emetic.
The People's power's a semblance of superstructure.
With a renewed passion, I too dream my own songs:
A prescription sealed above for enduring peace; and
Flavor, of a legacy carefully tailored to endure forever.

Violence in Silence by Roland Marke

Tenacity, as passion, sanctifies the chorus to empathy, chanting a mystic African chorus bids horror goodbye. Resilient females explode their hearts kissing the ground. They are little girls, teenagers, grown, ailing, old women: they appear helpless, powerless, against their assailants. Yet, despite their status, they are seized, openly raped, again and again; hate exploited a sacrilege of innocence: and still they sing of their agony, seeking self-esteem to steady their souls, the harmony bites to unmask misery in suffering. Cowards as trains only derail womanhood. Their rooted spirit's daring and steadfast as lighted eyes, and hearts sing their tears away. Song blooms comfort, as each soul seeks redemption. Poor older woman said, "Ruthless men have assaulted our bodies, not our spirit, we're fearless, vocal, stigmatized outcasts our society detest us. Prayer for justice unveils violence in silence."

My Mother Does Not Know...
By Osman Sankoh (Mallam O)

Does she know what day today is?
Does she know when it was agreed on?
Does she know who took the decision and why?
Does she know what to do today?
Does she know that some women are fighting for her rights?
Does she know that today is a day for women's voices to be heard?
What does 'general awareness for women' mean to her?

Yes, my mother in the village has accepted it that long.
To her, it is quite normal.
Was there, is there and will there be an
alternative to male control of female?
She has never tried to answer this question.
She does not have time to think about it.
Suppression or oppression of women, what does it mean?
Her children must be fed, daily.
That's important.

Women, Men and Country

In the morning.
As I was in my mother's womb in Africa,
I saw my mother hold a hoe;
I saw a bowl on her head;
I heard her talking to my brother on her back,
As she galloped us a mile barefooted to the farm.
She made a bed for him and gave him something to eat.
My brother did not see my smile as we were leaving him.
I prayed to God to protect him.

As my mother bent down to sow some seeds,
I saw an ant take away the first.
I told my mother but she was humming a song.

In the afternoon.
She gathered a few sticks to make fire.
It was very hot.
She went to the hut,
Where my brother was asleep, tired of crying.
She made food, hurriedly.
I didn't know why.
She ran with me around to gather some wood;
She picked up my brother,
Put the bunch of firewood on her head,
And galloped us quickly home.

In the evening.
It became clear to me why she was in a hurry.
My father was attending a meeting somewhere,
In a village close by.
He should find food at home on his return.
Oh men of Africa!
Why not be a bit more reasonable,
To my mother who is carrying me all the way?

It is true that my father also did some work,
But he always had it easy to walk to the farm.
He would hold a machete and that's all,
He would stop on the way to discuss the politics
of the village with friends.
My mother had me, my brother and a bowl or something else.
In the morning,
In the afternoon,
And in the evening.

Women, Men and Country

On this day,
I think about my mothers, my sisters, my aunts and all women,
Especially in Africa and elsewhere in the 'Muslim' world;
Especially those who still have it like my mother;
Those who spend all day looking after their children;
Those who must stay in backyards when decisions are to be taken;
Those whose office is 'destined' to be the kitchen;
Those who have just accepted things that way;
But also those who want things to change.

On this day,
As you 'enlightened' women try to make your voices heard,
I stand up to give you my support.
You may not hear or see what I do,
But you surely will!
My wife and daughters will join you in your fight,
"One day is one day".

But equally on this day,
I still ask myself a number of questions:
Why do you 'enlightened' women allow your dress to fall down easily,
In stupid scenes in films, on TV, etc.?
Why do you ask the authorities to accept prostitution as an occupation?
Because of some of these things,
It is a difficult fight you have ahead of you.
So please start right here in the West.

Mystery World Of Mystery People
By Foyre Jalloh

Why were we so different 400 years ago?
Did the melanin in our skin make us so different?
Why do we always have to stand out?
What makes my land different from your land?
Why should we fear?

Why should we not think for ourselves?
Why does our heritage make your heritage so different from ours?
My culture - the African Culture.
We can create our own future.
We're not blind we just can't see it yet.
We're not deaf, to not hear what you have to say about it.
We've made our history and without us your history wouldn't exist.
Our culture is like water, a form of peace travelling through war.
Water; a million crystals put together as one.
Once in our lives we were a dove in a cage, sooner or later we're a dove in the glare of your eyes, in the mist of the blue heaven.
We are our own culture; we peel the banana of mysteries.
We all wear our identity like a price tag.

We Sierra Leoneans wear our identity, like we dance our Gbondokali.
You Ghanaians wear your identity like you dance your Azonto

You Nigerians wear your identity like you dance your Atilogu

You British Africans wear your identity, like you drop the t out of wa'er.

You African Americans wear your identity, like the United States of Africa.

Sometimes we black girls and yes I mean our black girls use make-up as an identity,
the make-up to cover up the natural beauty.
Can you not see the pity that lay beneath, within and around the foundation of our
culture, our tradition?
We African girls wear our identity, like an African attire.
Ar taya, Ar taya.. I'm worn out like a tyre,
but my identity doesn't wear out, because I'm always wearing it.
If you combine this together it makes me. It makes you. It makes us.
I make up the kingdom of Africa in my head and I call that my home.
But this is only half of my story, maybe you can tell half of your story.

Khadi Mansaray

Part II: WOMEN

FOR VALERIE by Eldred Durosimi Jones

Measure her life, not in meandering minutes

But that intensity which raised her simple acts

To sacraments of service born of love.

She shed a radiating light which linked one heart to others, all to hers

To cast an ever-widening glow

Transcending barriers of country, kin and class.

Assuredly there is a source beyond the reach of understanding

From which such goodness flows with such abundance.

Some find this store through priestly intervention, altars, beads;

She touched the flame at all point of her life,

And passed the influence on.

The lives she beautified by her ennobling gift

Shall be her immortality;

Our full response of warmth her living scroll.

Woman by Hassan Arouni

Woman is
God's holy workshop
Co-creator.
Woman is love
cradle of Mankind,
Bosom of life.
Because Woman Is
I am.

I Hear A Woman Cry by Khadi Mansaray

Every day I hear a woman cry
I hear her sobs and feel her pain
I wonder what makes her cry
Disappointment or frustration
Accusation or damnation
I never know the reason why
But everyday I hear a woman cry

My Pains, Our World by Isata Mahoi

Why can't I be happy like other children
Why must I be the one to cry day and night,
Searching and yearning for that true love of parents,
People tell me to do things, things that I don't love doing.
They force me to do things ,that makes me regret living
Awful things that hurt so badly, scary way to live in this world
Giving me this weird feeling, feeling that I don't like
Feelings that make me regret being a girl.
Makes me think, if I were to be born again in this world,
I will prefer being a boy!
My heart is heavy, my mind is full
Crying and praying are my only solace;
I always wish to cry no more and end this misery,
But oooh, I always feel the pain, pain that hurts so badly;
Ooh, how I wish I could wake up to no more pains,
Maybe I should be more stronger and try not to cry
Stronger and stronger to fight against the monster
Too bad, other girls feel the same way too;
We should fight to survive; survive and fight to end it all
Maybe there is someone who cares;
Someone that can help us fight and fight and fight;

Dreams of a Girl-Mama by Akwasi Aidoo

*My genderless dreams of ascent won't be
deferred by teen missteps that have filled my body
heavy, shaken my brain into turmoil, stricken
my heart with anguish…*

*Not the dream of my own sweet embrace
of books bigger than my head and
schooling beyond the limits to create shades
of dignity for the stuck poor*

*Not the dream of a future without nightmares marring
the will to grow out of the trough under eaves
named poverty, nor dreams yet unborn to ride
the indomitable spirit the ancestresses bequeathed*

*Me to go the path from Sa Lone to the ends of
the world in peace and freedom for all girls and
to read and write in poetic license to the summits
of Fourah Bay with pedestrial anchor on terra cotta*

*My genderless dreams,
strong like morning batu, won't be
deferred now or ever, for nothing
but nothing will deter me!*

A Sense of Direction by Zeena Hamady

Freedom just lost it's wings
A barbed wire choked your rose
The sun burned Eden to ashes
Blocking what was once the path that i chose
Legends live forever
until one day they die
Love was said to conquer all
until one day it made a mother cry
Gravity dragged the whole world down
Until the human decided to fly
And the path that i was given
Made all my memories mine
A papercut slit my throat
A bird's feather caused my fall
After nature decided it had been nice enough
It hurled a whirlwind at me to demolish all

I Refuse by Khadi Mansaray

I Refuse to let you break me
I Refuse to let you take me
I Refuse to let you beat me
I Refuse to let you stop me
I Am Woman
And I Refuse

A Beauty, A Mother, A Mentor
By Agnes K Dugba Macauley

Women are soft, kind beautiful and bold
they are brave but too scared to be old
they have mighty brains which they use without knowing
and in difficult times, they multi task without groaning
with only two hands
she holds several hands
doing the work of a teacher
and also as a good preacher

She goes about in quiet times
doing her work with no smile
working tired, round the clock
while the ticks go on her clock

Then finally she retires
when her bones scream we are tired
It dawns on her that its not just about babies
but brains to educate herself to have other hobbies
to not limit herself to just baby sitting
but move to work and help build bigger cities
then finally limit her desire for just having them babies.

Dance of Life by Khadi Mansaray

Some people Waltz through life
Floating in beauty and romance
But all I do is Tango

Some people Jive through life
With joyful feet and happy beats
But all I do is Tango

Some Foxtrot through life
With quick, urgent and elegant steps
But all I do is Tango

My life is like the Tango
A constant flow of challenge
Intriguing and sarcastic

With passionate twists and elegant turns
Never easy but always awesome
Yes all I do is Tango

This Poem is for Her by Fatou Wurie

This Poem is for the girl who like a missing tooth was invisibly visible
Left on the sidewalk to cascade heated tears so hard it made the sun go fuck shine for the day.
This poem is for the girl who is too thick, so slick, to thin, to smart, to pretty, too un pretty too colored, too black, too white, too brown, too woman all too soon.
This is for the girl whose front tooth like the future that lies between the past and present stood gaped and half full.
This is for the girl whose color was too dark like the marmite spread her mama would saturate on white bread,
Her mahogany skin not wanted
Shunned in the nicest way possible
Exotic but not normal
Tolerated but not honored
Accepted but not loved
This is for her bleached dreams

Women, Men and Country

These words are for the girl whose body was too supple and refined
a girl's soul cased in a woman's body
as he rubbed his penis on her clitoris
softly at first..
leisurely as he pleasured him self-only
kneaded her tits like bread
    divided her legs like the second coming of Moses between red waters
for his pleasure-only

this is for girl whose front teeth stood imperfectly gaped
so we mocked her un-beauty-ness
for it was unconventional
it was African-ness
we robbed her of her smile
her confidence
her sense of self
her roots
her malnourished spirit became the slate
onto which we poured our own insecurities
and so she belies and belittles herself
cause we did not mirror her beautiful back to her
now she does not smile wide and bright
she stands a little crookedly
just like her front teeth
this is for the girl....
This is for that girl
This is for this girl

This is for the girls.
Girls,
Girls.

Because we did not say it enough
Because we did not say it loudly
Because we did not say it at all

So we start today in this lyrical delivery
(sing)
You are beautiful
You are beautiful
You beam this light on my skin
You queen

You are beautiful
Girl.

EDUCATING THE GIRL by Peagie Woobay

You educate a Child,
You educate a Nation.
You educate a Girl,
You educate the World.

For the girl Child,
Becomes a woman,
Then a mother.
A mentor and Educator.

One with patience and love,
Capable of doing multitasks.
A woman she becomes,
And thus a powerful driver of Progress

THE EYES OF A WOMAN by Peagie Woobay

Be it green, blue, black or brown like mine,
They say a lot that can be devine.
The EYES of a woman speak,
And describe her mood at every peak.
When in love, her eyes,
Shine, spark, stare and go tender,
Very sharp and caring they glister,
Sending out the warmth and love only a woman can send.
When sad her eyes go cold,
And glaze and burn but remain bold,
They pierce like a spy,
Questioning why.
When angry they grow wide,
Like fire they spark and go wild,
Showing anger and rage,
Though controlled at every stage.
And when deceived,
The eyes of a woman receive,
Laceration effects, like erosions,
Of the hillside of Mama Salone.

THE STRENGTH OF A WOMAN
By Peagie Woobay

Twas one day in March,
The sun burnt high in LAND THAT WE LOVE,
Yet her part of the world was cold and dark with snow,
Then came April and spring, the beginning of life,
Out of the blues something was born.
The flowers grew and the poet wrote,
Each poem praised her beauty, intelligence and strength.
May came with more poems,
Each one making the subject of the poems,
Though an enigma, bloom and fall in love.
Burning and wishing to see the poet…..
She waits…..

THE TEARS OF A WOMAN by Peagie Woobay

They flow from her heart.....
Expressing exactly what they should. ...
Can be of sadness.....
Can be of happiness. ......

Her tears remain genuine as can be…..

And when the tears dry up….
She moves on……
To a better woman…..
And loves from the heart…..

THE SMILES OF A WOMAN by Peagie Woobay

-Her smile, so full
Comes from her heart
With a bright future ahead
Fooling no one........

-Her smile, so full
Sparks with love
That no man has
And reaches out
Loving someone.......

-Her smile, so full
Keeps her going
Keeps her loving
Keeps her doing
Yet hurting no one.......

Elegance by Janice Williams

*In the small village of Ndebele, South Africa
the women wear beautiful gold neck rings that accumulate
as the years go on. Such terms as the "giraffe women"
have been given to them. In a way
they are very much like giraffes --
with their long, graceful necks.*

*I remember going back home to the motherland
and witnessing something new;
young girls of the village, with their head ties wrapped
and gold glimmering, carried big buckets of water
from the well, early in the morning before the sun came up.
Were they there before and I just didn't see them?
I don't know, but I pretended that
nothing I saw fazed me.*

*He was ignorant, always badgering the elders
to get rid of the rings because he was a western doctor
and knew it all.*

Her Beauty by Janice Williams

Hers is not of the beautiful actress
whose shapely body produces whistles
and cheers from the men and
from the women? deadly jealous looks,
as dark as the unlit part of the galaxy.

Hers is not that of Ms. America's
who glides across the stage effortlessly
with a smile brilliant enough to light the world.

Hers is not as rare as the beautiful diamonds
now scarcely found on the African continent,
after the red land had been washed clean of its exquisiteness.

Hers is not of the beauty of magic, which
is so carefully watched and handled.

Hers is that of a nurse, whose caring hands
erase the fears and pains of the ailing.

Hers is that of the writer, whose well-crafted words
touch the depths of many hearts, leaving remarkable tattoos.

Hers is that of the rising sun, which delicately paints the sky
with its magnificent light.

Hers is that of the beautiful lion mountains
of Sierra Leone which cannot be taken in all at once.

Hers...could be said to be greater.

Stirred by Janice Williams

His fingers crawl up my stomach.
Making unbearable, tingling sensations
that reach all the way up
to my chest.

There goes that chill again. My voice is gone.
I don't know if I can move my body.
What's next to stand still,
but my heart hammering within?

My eyes can't shut any tighter.
I take my last breath, before
he overtakes me.

My knuckles go white
as I hold on to the covers with dear
life.

The angel I once knew
spreads his darkness and steals my soul.

Undefined by Janice Williams

I want you to see that I
am the struggle within the river;
rushing, circling dancing
on the waters and rocks.

I find myself breathing in rhythm
to the beats of the waves.
Sometimes its a solemn march;
a clop, clap, clack
crescendo.

Don't set off the alarm
and bring out the villagers when
I am sharp as the dog's bark.
I can be the silence of
a lover's secret.

I will not be a Stepford or Desperate housewife
consumed by Pride and Prejudice.
I will be soft, sweet and waiting
as the passing city in
the late night.

Part III: MEN

MEN by Peagie Woobay

God made them in his own image,
They can be sweet but with a lot of baggage.

Their shoulders can be of support
But also of distort.

They lead and mislead,
But yet we love them,
For without them a woman is sometimes lost.

Their strength, we sense in their muscles,
And look up to them without scruples.

May God keep them in His image,
So women can add them to their adage.

Oh heart o' mine; Oh heart... are you mine?
By Achieng Maureen Akena

If you are mine, why does he beat you so fast
If you are mine, why does he make you burst
If you are mine, why don't I control your beat
If you are mine, why can't I control your heat

Oh heart, oh heart tell me true
If you are mine, why does he make you blue
If you are mine, why can't I keep you calm
When he comes by, why do you sound the alarm

Oh heart, oh heart do you really know
Where you belong, and who you owe
If you did, if you did, you would not stop
He would not make you flip flop

Oh heart, for sure, I guarantee
That if you were mine, beating for me
He would not break you with his eye
Then leave you out to bleed and die

Oh heart, oh heart I beseech you
Don't let me down, don't be a fool
For if you keep up with this banging

He will find me where I am hiding

Am I A Boy? by Khadi Mansaray

I long for the mother
That I had to kill
I long for toys
But I hold a gun
I have blood on my hands
Instead of books
They say a man protects his own
But am I a man?
Or am I a boy?

Grandfather by Rahmatullah Mansaray

May your soul rest in peace
Uncle Hassani is already here
Hoping to get you ready
As they call the Azan
My joy at seeing your face
May Allah bless you child you say
All your wishes will be granted
Daily you will be blessed

May all hopeless days disappear
Allah be with you
Hold on to your faith
Do your prayers
Inshallah all will be well

She Simply Looks Simple by Fatou Wurie

In melody
He is allowed to enter

starting into her
his face is capped with pleasure
She simply looks simple.

Puddles.
She jumps into the puddle
Deeper than expected
Just like her hole.

Thrusting
Wider,
She un-becomes
he dances, latching at control.

They both fall into tangled cosmic imbalances.

It is winter
The chills aren't very kind,
She steadily smokes her cigarettes,
Drags real slow
memories pouring real fast,
rapid rapidly.

she continues to inhale
he exhales
 in his sleep.

Bitch.
He whispers sweet nothings into her ear stream
Her name is uncomplicated
Sit down,

Women, Men and Country

Be good.
He doesn't notice she has a dog.

His mouth is greedy for her breasts
She simply looks simple.

THE SUPERIOR RACE by Eldred Durosimi Jones

Where is this superior race?
Not that rabid, slavering mob,
Faces distorted in hate, bodes distorted with violence.
Hurling brickbats, cursing priest, kicking newsmen.

A student alight from a railway coach,
Awaits his transport in the waiting room,
And for this time crime, he has his teeth knocked out
By men who thus assert superior nature.

A band of students in a southern street
Silently walking two abreast
Protest the violation of a fellow student.
From either curb the violators hurl abuse and stones.
Still they walk on, proud in their humiliation.

Some knock out teeth,
Others excel in curses, some spread insidious lies,
All abound in hate, all steeped in the past.

Women, Men and Country

Empty men who having nothing else, fall back on whiteness.

A line of student white as well coloured,
Silently picket a segregated movie house.
All white once dare to leave the snugness of their whiteness
The coloured shake off the years of acquiescence.
Silently they strive to elevate mankind.

They have dared to leave the safety of the great white hill;
They have dared to leave the smugness of the arid black vale;
The have met in sober reason, on middle ground,
Here to do battle in the cause of human man.

These who have nothing to gain except their souls,
Nothing to lose, except their bodies' comfort,
These who have risen in a greater cause than pigmentation,
These are superior- they are men.

Khadi Mansaray

Part IV: COUNTRY

Horizontal Green-White-Blue*
by Claudia Anthony

let green stimulate our land fertile
for God to us it hath endowed
our resources vast, rich bestowed
bitter pill: handouts for which we file

let white reveal glitters of diamonds
on a queen's crown without her toil
extracted gratis from our affluent soil
by missionaries I name vagabonds

let it also for her bootlickers be, far
still rooted on this precious land of ours
she like them from evasive peace showers
to leave in char Athens of West Africa

let blue be for our multitudinous seas
all lives in and under them; even virgin
enough to make us self-sufficient lasting
for God to us them in creation concedes

from which alien pirates trespass, flourish
so till cows come home we keep knocking
for breading, fishing, graining and milking
all what God to us in creation did furnish

Our Own Place by Josephine Coker

Yes we will showcase
That we have a place
There, a sweet solace
Where yet we find grace

For after we've flown
Oh yes we do roam
In moments alone
We remember our Home

We have electricity
In another's country
We're even given liberty
To ebb and flow with levity

We rear a fresh breed
Even with great ease
They do as they please
Still we'll never cease

To yearn and pine
For our sweet palm wine,
For cassava leaves to dine
And yester voices divine.

So to heed the call
Of the dancing stalls
And the hawking calls
We retreat to Mother All

THE PLACE by Peagie Woobay

The Place is just where you want to be…..
The Place is just where you won't leave…..

The Atlantic waves bring peace to the Place……
Letting you relax in peace at the Place…..

A blend of African and European touch…..
Gives you the feeling there's none like such…..

Reviving tourism in all its glory…..
Nature in abundance to bury your worries…..

Yeniva and crew make you happy…..

Land That We Love, by Peagie Woobay

My devotion to you is not political,
It is all sincere and national.

My love for you surpasses all,
With a passion that is unending.

For the glory I give to you, Oh, Lion Mountains,
Is one that never tires.

My dreams, my dreams, I put in action,
For thee oh land that I love.

Mena Hills By Marie Forna

Easy to ascend but difficult to descend
Once up you experience the cool breeze blowing over Makeni
It can be slippery like….
You have to be careful so you don't fall
The beauty of the hills represents the beauty of Women
Who live their daily lives making the world a better place

Sierra Leone, The Beauty of a Nation
By Peagie Woobay

Green, White and Blue, flow in my blood
Everywhere I go they run through my veins.
The Lion Mountains, ever so beautiful engulf me
Each time I go not wanting to leave.

The smiling kids all over get my brilliant warm smiles in return.
The white lengthy sandy beaches, I linger on for long.
The Sherbro islands draw me close.
The burning humid heat refreshes my root and I cling to it.

But why, oh why? Mama Salone. Why…
Do your people suffer?
And go to bed in the dark?

The Lion by Abibatu Samura

*Finally, the lion was released
from its cage. By now it was iced
with its reddish brittle coating,
that had left the lion isolated,
kept it captive for centuries
that passed by like foreign tourists.
On this dry sand the lion
ran widely without the
buoyancy of the clouds carrying
it through the dusty desert.
But this did not faze the lion,
for it took almost eternity
for its fight to freedom.
Years of living in darkness
its glowing golden fur, covered
in the cold black dirt,
searching for the white
lustrous stone that had made
false promises of seeing
the light of freedom.
The aggressive, burning
light this lion had prayed to
see for years greeted it
as an old friend.
For the sun had long-awaited for
the lion's return.*

*Now the lion had ran
from its blacks and greys,
into the greens, whites and blues
to reunite its colours
"Mighty they made thee"
onto the mountains, high
to release that destined roar.*

The Flag of Sierra Leone by Abibatu Samura

*Green: I feel the land God has created
I see the nature we shall care for
The world is in our care*

*White: Freedom and surrender
The good path we shall follow
To show us the right way
Clean and simple, like how God sees us*

*Blue: The sky above me gives
Me sunshine and rain
The sea below me gives me gives
Me water to drink, to clean, to live on*

*The flag of Sierra Leone,
Oh wise colours they are.
Colours God has made for man
Green, white and blue are the
Special colours* for you!

My Land! My Home! My Country!
by Chadia Talib

My Land, My Home My Country..
the only place I know..
Tucked away on the West Coast..
With God's Glory to show..
Beautiful hills, breathtaking shores..
and wonderful people too..
My Land, My Home, My Country..the only place I know..
I've walked the Earth and sailed the seas ..
and visited every port..None as good and warm and free..as
this tiny land to see..
My Land, My Home, My Country..
Oh ! how I treasure thee..
palms and nuts and gold and ore..
a blessing like Heaven's door..
My Land, My Home, My Country..
need I call your name?..
The wind and echo of the hills..
will surely beckon thee..
I hear the whisper and overwhelming stir..
of sand and dust and leaves..
Yes !! Its You !!..
My Golden Land..
My haven..
SIERRA LEONE !!..

Bunce Island by Roland Marke

*Amid the rumbling Sierra Leonean waters,
Enveloped into the deep of Atlantic Ocean,
Stood this dark and mighty fortress, called
Bunce Island: that caricatures the-Bastille,
Dark-dungeon to stockpile African slaves:
History sleeps here like the one-eyed man.
Around 1700s -1800s, our ancestors were
Chained, forced to a ˜Point of no Return,'
At a warehouse of humanity, and waiting
Shipment onto Charleston, Savannah in
The South or New York in United States;
Gullahs from beloved home worked rice
Farms in South Carolina: the grim trade's
Intertwined with blemished history of UK,
United States and motherland Sierra Leone:
Neither time nor distance, would triumph:
To eradicate this gloomy enduring legacy.*

Nelson Mandela by Roland Marke

Legendary icon, injustice personified
Epitomizes Africa's indicted ancestry
Apartheid's homegrown dehumanization
Branded criminal, whim, baseless crime
Essence of freedom liberation or death
Did carry cross, lifetime crown he wears
Robust inspiration celebrated unification
Africa wears the face of Nelson Mandela
Empowerment immortal and unshakable
Wedged a clear dent on wall of freedom
Symbol of heroism an electric inspiration
Like eloquent poetry he's a living peace
His silence made detractors nothingness
Institutionalized as a malignant cancer
Xenophobia and exploitation married
Beacon of freedom knew no violence
Equality dignity eventually resurrected
Africa, strive to emulate ailing Mandela.

Managed directly by God from Heaven
by Linda Ochiel

the Mara
legions of wildebeest and zebra
stream across the tawny Savanna...
fording the Mara River in perpetual search for pasture
indeed, a vibrant ribbon of life,
Meandering...

this quiet intimacy....
this part of my heritage, I must only share with you
my friend...
because you deserve it
also because between idle talk and reality,
this is the untainted best
Imagine
wildlife ranging from pods of hippo, to prides of lion
crouching in ambush
along vegetated banks of the Mara...
the rivers' bird life is spectacular
and patient watchers will indeed
be rewarded with sightings of kingfisher.

don't worry about the disemboweled airport
in the vast country such as mine
why would you lack a plain to land your plane?

Really?
Questions on who or what started the fire
or how fast such a tiny fire such as that spread

are immaterial, my love
in any case, can any fire be tiny?
you see, my countrymen are very optimistic
why emergency preparedness?
we don't build airports for fire...
or should we?

and in any case, this beautiful country of mine,
like Pakistan, is managed directly by God from heaven
How do you think we have survived for this long?

Unconventional? by Linda Ochiel

From this panoramic perch
A top Lake Naivasha, I savor one of human kind's oldest views
Over the sweeping floor of the largest valley
A flashback

Severing the garland of the dos and don'ts,
Foisted on us for generations
Prying open the clenched fist of norms and roles
A diseased antagonism appropriated for us
A pander to the expectations of the sanctimonious…

A leader? Young, unmarried and childless?
Unconventional!

Then, the sputter and rage
Amidst jubilation at my coronation
The people have spoken!

A smile at the moon and wink at the sun
Rolling over and over the dewy grass
Shoeless, in a tie
Full of laughter and promise
I transmute into an 'honorable'
Overnight

Memories of 28 by Khadi Mansaray

Memories of 28 etched in my mind
My eyes open to the sound of the Azan
From the mosque next door
I watered the flowers and opened the gates

Memories of 28 etched in my mind
Apple tree, mango tree
Banana and palm
Not forgetting hellfire plums

Memories of 28 etched in my mind
Weddings, births and burials
Awujoh pots ruled
Sheep and Cows fattened for Eid

Memories of 28 etched in my mind
Chickens slaughtered for lunch
Friends and family Mama would feed
Princes and paupers Papa's counsel heed

Memories of 28, etched in my mind
Slaves in uniform bring their fire
Our lifetime and history goes up in flames
Yet from the ruins we rebuilt

Memories of 28, etched in my mind
The joys of childhood
The pains of war
And the ultimate victory of survival

Part V: HAIKU CORNER

A SELECTION OF HAIKUS BY KHADI MANSARAY

SALONE
Fertile soils! gold and diamonds flow!
But my people
Make me flee to empty foreign lands

THE LAND
Gives us crops so we may live
And holds our corpses
When we are done

THE SEA
With dolphins and sharks, the wonders of creation
Angry waves
Bring death and destruction

THE WIND
Over land and sea, I move and rule
You choose
Gentle breeze or angry storm

LOVE
Content and happy, in your embrace
Cut
Heartbreak and sorrow now replace

MEET THE POETS

Abdul Tejan-Cole
Abdul Tejan-Cole is Executive Director of OSIWA. Prior to his appointment, Abdul served as Commissioner of the Anti-Corruption Commission in Sierra Leone, Abdul's previous positions include: Attorney in the Special Court for Sierra Leone; Deputy Director for the International Center for Transitional Justices' (ICTJ) Cape Town Office; and President of the Sierra Leone Bar Association. Abdul also has extensive experience working with Open Society Institute (OSI). He served as Board Chair of OSIWA, and has also served as a member of the board of the Open Society Justice Initiative (OSJI).

Abibatu Samura
An aspiring poet, Abibatu Samura was born in London to Sierra Leonean parents. Currently living in Coventry, England, she attends the Bishop Ullathorne Catholic, reading History, Drama, Philosophy and Ethics and Sociology. She recently passed her GCEs with flying colours. Speaking about her inspiration as a poet, Abibatu said, "I think it was discovering more about Sierra Leone's history and the country in general that made me want to write poems about it"

Achieng Achena
Achieng Maureen Akena from Kenya is a human rights and democracy practitioner who has worked around Africa with different institutions. She is a lawyer, a poet, a woman, and an adventurer in life.

Ade Daramy

Ade Daramy is a Sierra Leonean journalist and broadcaster, poet, social commentator, motivational speaker and media trainer. He is a cultural commentator on modern popular culture, with a passion for the history of music, sports and African and World politics. He has worked with the BBC World Service, currently co-edits the quarterly Journal of Sierra Leone Studies and edits Promota Africa. He also presents, My World of Music on Colourful Radio in the UK. He previously edited Mano Vision, a Sierra Leonean magazine and the British Government's magazine 'Modernising Government News'. He has written for many other publications over the years. Ade is an authority on Africa and Sierra Leone's history and culture. He is also the former chairman of the Sierra Leone Diaspora Network (UK) and an ambassador for FORWARD an African Diaspora women's campaign and support charity (registered in the UK).

Agnes K Dugba Macauley

Agnes was born in Kono District, Sierra Leone she learnt Italian and Administration in Milan and short hand and secretariat duties in London. She has worked for the Sierra Leone and Zambia embassies in Brussels and was a Case Administrator at the London Probation Trust from 1999 to 2010. Agnes loves reading and writing songs and poems. She is happily married to Charlie Ojukutu-Macauley and a proud mother of three sons.

Akwasi Aidoo

Dr. Akwasi Aidoo is the founding Executive TrustAfrica, a foundation dedicated to inclusive development and democratic gove Africa. He is also the Chair of the Boards of ..source Alliance, Fund for Global Human Rights, and Open Society Initiative for West Africa (OSIWA). Akwasi has taught at universities in Ghana, Tanzania, and the United States. He was educated in Ghana and the United States and received a Ph.D. in medical sociology from the University of Connecticut. He writes poetry and short stories in his spare time.

Chadia Talib

Chadia Talib is an entrepreneur living in Bo, Southern Sierra Leone. She is also a freelance writer and passionate about Women's issues.

Claudia Anthony

Claudia Anthony is an award winning media practitioner with publications in journals in Germany and South Africa. In Sierra Leone she is the Founder and Executive publisher of Tribune of the People and founder of the Alliance for Female Journalists. She has been a journalist on three local newspapers and is the Germany Bureau editor for Expo times. Her freelance work includes BBC World Service Network and Radio Deutsche Welle. Claudia was the senior radio producer for the BBC World Service on the Charles Taylor trial and is currently the African Bureau editor for Voices from the Diaspora Radio Network. Her awards include Hellman Hammett Journalism Prize in 2000, the NOVIB PEN Award and the Outstanding Media Practitioner of the year 2010 by Independent Media Commission Sierra Leone.

Christopher Dawah Sese Koker
Dawah Sese Koker also known as *The Oracle* is a sales person and describes himself as a self taught, half-baked-booked. A paradox persona he is traditional but not conventional.

David E Manley
David Emmanuel Maevan Manley has always loved words and guessing by his multitude of names, it's a feeling that runs in the family. Seduced by the different worlds open to exploration at a very early age on those Saturday mornings at the Sierra Leone Library Board, it was a pleasant surprise when his words started meandering out in pretty compositions. Presently living outside of Sierra Leone, David is still inspired by the memories of Sierra Leone and the stories of everyday Sierra Leoneans.

Fatou Wurie
Fatou is a communications and branding strategist and blogger. She holds a BA in political science and gender studies from the University of British Columbia (UBC). She is the CEO and managing director at Free{the}Town, a firm that specializes in branding for African projects. Her clients include UNICEF, Health Poverty Action (HPA), Sweet Salone and Sierra Leone National Shipping Carrier (SLNC) and she is the Comunications advisor at MamaYe. Fatou is also a TEDx Freetown organizer, a columnist at Standard Times Newspaper. Her work can be found on the fatoublog and Huffington Post. She is board member of OWNERS, a social entrepreneurial project that empowers local female owned businesses.

Eldred D Jones

Eldred Durosimi Jones is known internationally as being central to the study of African writing in the new universities of Africa, Britain and North America and is the founding editor of The Annual African Literature Today. His book Othello's Countrymen introduced Africa into Shakespeare studies. He was educated in two historic institutions of Equatorial Africa, the CMS Grammar School and Fourah Bay College and holds an M.A. Oxford and Ph.D Durham. He was successively Lecturer, Professor, Principal and Pro-Vice-Chancellor of Fourah Bay College University of Sierra Leone. He lost his sight in his middle years but continued to be an inspiring and outstanding person and became the founding Chairman of Sierra Leone Union on Disabilities Issues; His recently published memoirs, The Freetown Bond is an account of his remarkable life. Eldred Durosimi Jones is Emeritus Professor of English Language and Literature, a Fellow of the Royal Society of Arts, recipient of the Royal Society of Arts Silver Medal, Honorary Fellow, Corpus Christi College, Oxford, and joint winner (with Marjorie Jones) of the African Studies Association of the UK Distinguished Africanist Award.

Festy Natty

Nattyman, as friends fondly call him, is an accomplished poet. He is the author of SONG OF A BEACH. Born in Freetown Sierra Leone, he currently lives in the USA and is married with three sons. He loves playing Chess and Scrabble.

Fouad Ayoub
Fouad Ayoub is an entrepreneur, artist and poet. He was born in Freetown and went to school in Koidu. He studied arts and design in the university of Minnesota, Minneapolis.USA.

Foyre Jalloh
Foyre Jalloh is 13 years old. She is of Sierra Leone and Nigerian heritage born in United Kingdom. She has a keen interest in writing and performance arts and has already published three poems.

Isata Mahoi
Isata Mahoi was born in Moyamba District, Southern Sierra Leone. Presently pursuing a doctorate in Economic Policy at the Catholic University of Milan in Italy. She has a good background on project writing and management. She has worked at top management level in diverse fields of interest ranging from the rights of women and children, gender and development, democratic governance, and agriculture. She worked in the media in Sierra Leone and is also a performing artist. She likes working at grassroots level with the most vulnerable people and her strength lies in community out-reach.

Janice Williams
Janice is a Sierra Leonean living in the USA. As a young girl she enjoyed listening to her elders tell stories in her village and used to write stories in her mind to fall asleep. She studied Political Science, Communications and Creative Writing and loves poetry. Janice is a blogger and is working on a on a series of short stories, and an autobiography.

Josephine Coker

Josephine is a teacher, insurer and marketeer with a background spanning education, health and business sectors. She was a market analyst and brand development consultant, surviving several mergers at General Accident to work for the company that is now Aviva, a blue chip company in the financial services industry. She also worked as a marketing consultant in the public sector. She is currently pursuing a personal interest in the form of a law degree and is also a devoted mother. One of Josephine's passions is the development of Sierra Leoneans so they can help develop Sierra Leone.

Khadi Mansaray

Khadi Mansaray FCCA, was born in Sierra Leone and lives in London. She is a chartered accountant and with several years in Financial Services working for Direct Line Group and the Royal Bank of Scotland Group. She is a business coach and ambassador for Girl Child Network SL, as well as an NHS Expert Patient and contact for Lupus UK. Khadi is also a writer and journalist. She has written several articles on gender issues and is a regular contributor to GoWoman magazine and PoliticoSL newspaper. Her work has also appeared in other African publications including Shout Africa, Ghana Oracle, Patriotic Vanguard and Mano Vision. She is also the Children and Gender Editor, Vice President, UK producer and host of Voices from the Diaspora Radio Network. Khadi is a trustee for the Peagie Woobay Scholarship Fund and project manager of the Books not Babies initiative.

Linda Ochiel

Linda Ochiel is a seasoned poet, writer and documentary producer with regional and international experience in peace building, democracy, governance, and human rights. Currently she is a Director of Policy, Advocacy, and Communications at the Commission on Administrative Justice (Office of the Ombudsman) Kenya. Previously, she spearheaded national peace initiatives and was instrumental in the investigations and documentation of 2007/2008 post-election violence in Kenya. She has played an active role in pushing the previous regime to promote transitional justice, accountability, constitutional, and electoral reforms. She is instrumental in fighting against violations of women's rights, and statelessness; and in promoting citizenship, natural resource governance, and access to information at the regional and international levels. She wrote a column in the East African Standard focusing on women and children's rights and has produced a number of documentaries to expose human rights violations in Kenya. Among these include documentaries titled, 'In Search of My Land Rights' (advocating for women's rights to land as guaranteed in Kenya's constitution) and 'Robbed of Choice' (agitating for a stop to forced sterilization of HIV positive women in Kenya'. The documentaries are produced under pseudo name, Dana Nyogoda.

Marie Fornah

Marie is a sixteen-year-old JSS2 pupil and beneficiary of the Peagie Woobay fund. Mena Hills is her first poem and was written on Mena Hills.

Milton Margai

Milton is a freelance journalist and writer. He was a founding member of the Amnesty International Press Group (SL). He was encouraged to practice journalism by Hilton Fyle after submitting an impressive article for an essay competition held by Mr Fyle on his return to SL. He became Mr Fyle's protégé and never looked back. He currently resides in the UK. Milton is a social sciences and research graduate and has worked as a marketing/data analyst and researcher. Currently, Milton is focusing on his writing and working on his first book. He is a proud father who is passionate about human rights, development and good governance in Sierra Leone. He hosts and presents shows on the Voices from the Diaspora Radio Network. To Milton, it is nation first and all else is secondary.

Osman Sankoh

Osman Alimamy Sankoh (Mallam O.) is the Executive Director of the INDEPTH Network, an international NGO based in Accra, Ghana. Commonly known as Mallam O, he was born in Sierra Leone. He holds a B.Sc.Ed. from Njala University where he was Student Union President in 1985/86. He also studied at the University of Dortmund in Germany where he obtained a B.Sc. Hons, M.Sc. and D.Sc in Applied Statistics and was a scientist in the Department of Tropical Hygiene and Public Health at the University of Heidelberg, Germany. Mallam O. also taught at three secondary schools in Sierra Leone and was a Research/Teaching Assistant at NUC. He is the founding editor-in-chief of the international African Journal of Environmental Assessment and Management (AJEAM) and co-founder of Africa Positive, a magazine in Germany that portrays the positive sides of Africa. He has authored several books including "Hybrid Eyes - Reflections of an African in Europe", "Beautiful Colours - Reflections on the Problem of Racism", "Statistics Without Fear - Descriptive Statistics", "A New Method for the Analysis of Forestry Data", and "Climate Variability and Malaria Transmission Risk". Mallam O. is also founder and publisher of the Sierra Leonean

...eries, an initiative that gives opportunities to Sierra Leonean origin to publish their books.

Peagie Woobay
Peagie Woobay is the Founder and CEO of The Peagie Woobay Scholarship Fund. She studied Modern Languages at the University of Sierra Leone and Public Administration in Paris. Married with two kids, she currently lives in Stockholm and works at the embassy of Malaysia as Administrative and Finance Officer. Peagie speaks English, French and Swedish. She describes herself as a Sierra Leonean that carries Sierra Leone in her heart and takes it everywhere she goes.

Rahmatullah Mansaray
Rahmatullah was born in the UK but grew up in SL. She returned to UK in her teens as a result of the war. She studied Accounting and Finance at the University of Manchester and is a member of the Chartered Institute of Management Accountants. She has worked for media and real estate companies including Financial Times and Grosvenor Estate Management Ltd. She enjoys going to the theatre, listening to music and spending time with friends and family. 'Grandfather' is her first poem.

Roland Bankole Marke
Roland Bankole Marke is the author of two collections of poetry: Teardrops Keep Falling and Silver Rain and Blizzard. His third book is Harvest of Hate: Stories and Essays. He's deputy editor of Patriotic Vanguard, and writes commentaries, served as a columnist who reviews literature books. His poems and short stories have been anthologized in several anthologies. Roland's work has appeared in various journals and magazines, including Journal of the African Literature Association,

Pambazuka, Worldpress.org and African Sun Times. He lives and writes in Jacksonville, Florida, USA.

Zeena Hamady
Zeena Hamady is a Sierra Leonean of Lebanese descent, currently in Lebanon she carries Sierra Leone with her.